Massacre at Roanoke

The Destruction of a Georgia Town
An Incident in the Creek War of 1836

G.G. Stokes, Jr.

Printed in the United States of America

ISBN 13: 978-0615541563

ISBN 10: 0615541569

First printing 2011, Chattahoochee Publishing

Visit the Author's Website

www.GeorgiaWriter.com

Massacre at Roanoke

The Destruction of a Georgia Town
An Incident in the Creek War of 1836

Roanoke (1831-1836) is one of the forgotten towns in Georgia. Other than a few references in specialized history books such as *Georgia Place Names,*[1] or in the histories of some Georgia counties, there is little mention of it today. The few references found tell brief stories that tend to raise as many questions as they answer, such as: "On Friday, May 13, 1836, this Georgia town was attacked by Creek Indians who burned the town to the ground and murdered most of the inhabitants,"[2] or "Men, women, and children, armed and unarmed, alike were killed without mercy and scalped."[3]

Roanoke was founded in newly formed Stewart County in 1831 and incorporated on December 22, 1832. It was located on fifty acres of land purchased from Richard Mathias near the Chattahoochee River and was situated about a quarter of a mile from a river landing serving a nearby plantation.[4] The land had originally been part of a two-thousand acre tract belonging to General Robert Toombs. Prior to his ownership, it had been the location of an Indian town.[5] The original charter shows the name as Roan-Oak, but subsequent references refer to it as Roanoke.[6]

By 1836, Roanoke contained some twenty to thirty families, a river dock, and several stores.[7] These included: Joice's Store, Starke's Store,[8] Rood and Seymour's,[9] a post office,[10] Gibson and Williams cotton warehouse, Mathias and Son, Hill Brothers,[11] and Matthews and Son[12] which also served as a hotel.[13] Some sources state that there were actually two cotton warehouses located in the town.[14] There may have been other businesses located there, but the names are not preserved. According to one report, there were many fine mansions in the town prior to its destruction.[15]

The loss of their land through treaties signed by a minority of the tribe and other mistreatments by settlers led to a smoldering resentment among the Creeks that burst into open hostility in 1836.[16] A report to Brigadier General George Gibson from Captain John Page, the Superintendent of the Creeks, dated May 16, 1836, begins with the statement, "I discover the hostility extends further than I was aware of." In his report, Captain Page relays news of several engagements between settlers and Indians, including the news of the burning of Roanoke: "Seven persons were discovered dead by a person passing by this place. (Roanoke)". He also reported that the town and a steamboat were burned.[17]

The Indians may have attacked Roanoke because it was located on a site previously occupied by an Indian village and they resented the fact that the settlers had crowded them out of land they considered their own.[18] Another possibility is that there may have been a shallow ford, or at least a well-known one, located nearby.[19] This seems likely, as there were Creek scouts appearing and disappearing at intervals before and after the attacks of May 13th and 15th.

Although the Creek War that erupted in 1836 was a major uprising, only about one-fifth of the Creeks joined in the fighting. Estimates put the total number of participants at five-thousand, most of which came from the Hitchiti, Chehaw, Eufaula, and Uchee villages of Lower Creeks located across the Chattahoochee River from Roanoke, in Alabama. Members of the Uchee tribe were late comers to the uprising. Two black men captured at Roanoke, who later escaped, stated that the Hitchiti were unable to solicit help from the Uchee during the time that they were held prisoners.[20]

There were three main groups of hostiles. One group was led by Eneah Mathla who was the overall leader of the uprising, a second group was led by Eneah Micco who was the recognized head chief of the Lower Creeks, and the third group was led by an avid anti-removal leader known as Jim Henry.[21] Jim Henry's group is credited with the attack on Roanoke.

Four-fifths of the Creek nation remained friendly to the Americans during the war, supplying 1,806[22] warriors to assist the United States.[23] Many of these same warriors later aided the United States in the fight against their Seminole cousins in Florida. Their pay was supplemented by funds realized from the capture and resale of blacks captured among the hostiles.[24]

The first attack on Roanoke began Friday night, May 13, 1836, when Creek warriors attacked the steamer *Georgian* on the Chattahoochee River. According to early reports they killed everyone on board except for the ship's engineer.[25] Another Steamer, the *Hyperian*,[26] was attacked two miles up river. At least four crew members were killed before the captain and two women made their escape. Left adrift, the vessel later grounded on a sandbar in the river.[27] An early report stated that the *Georgian* was burned and about thirty warriors who attacked the town were repulsed, but later accounts held that the *Georgian* had been able to "get off" and escape without loss of life after the firing had commenced.[28]

The town had a blockhouse and several settlers had been posted as pickets prior to the attack.[29] While some of the settlers withdrew under the direction of the Army,[30] a company of Stewart County militia under the command of

Captain James Uriah Horne[31] stayed to keep an uneasy watch the following Saturday.[32] Approximately forty to fifty people remained in the town. All of the women and children except for a Mrs. Kershaw and her infant child[33] were removed to the safety of the town of Lumpkin. Including local civilians and the militia who remained with them, the town contained sixty to seventy people at the time of the Sunday morning attack.[34]

When nothing alarmed the defenders on the night of May 14th, they retired to their camp located near one of the warehouses in town.[35] In his reminiscence about the burning of Roanoke, written fifty years after the battle and published in the Americus, Georgia, *Daily Republican*, Joseph John Granberry stated that the pickets, not anticipating any immediate attack, retired to their camp and lay down to sleep. Although Granberry was not in the town at the time of the attack, he had been there on Friday, at which time he had been convinced to join the troop of militia guarding the town. After returning home to advise his father of this decision, he was on his way back Sunday morning when he met a fleeing mob of people who told him that Captain Horne's company had been killed and scalped, and that the town had been burned to ashes.[36] He does not say where he obtained his information about the sleeping pickets, but in light of the complete surprise attained by the attackers, it is highly probable that he was correct. Another report states that the night before the attack "the woods surrounding the town were filled with the hooting of owls, beginning at a distance and drawing nearer. It developed later that the Indians were using this call for their signal as they closed in on all sides."[37]

Just before dawn[38] on Sunday morning, May 15, 1836, the inhabitants of Roanoke were awakened by the sounds of gunfire. Any picket who had remained on his post was quickly overrun by a force of about three hundred Creek warriors as they rushed the town. An eyewitness account was given by Colonel Felix G. Gibson, who was asleep in his home. Colonel Gibson[39] tells of being awakened by the sounds of gunfire and springing to his feet just as three Indians thrust their guns through the window and fired into his bed. He immediately grabbed his own weapon, a double-barreled shotgun, and attempted to escape through the front door, but found it blocked. Racing through his home amid a torrent of gunfire directed at him from every window in his house, he attempted to flee through another door, but was shot at by two attackers outside of his house. Slamming the door shut, he opened it again and fired out into the yard before making a dash for safety. Miraculously, he escaped into the surrounding woods with only a cut on his nose,[40] powder burns on his clothing, and a bruise sustained when he was hit or clubbed as he ran through a crowd of warriors who were more intent on looting and burning than in killing him. His brother-in-law, Gazaway Williams, sleeping upstairs, was able to leap through a window and escape unharmed.

Two brothers named Donaldson, also in the Gibson house, were killed and their bodies consumed by flames when the Indians fired the structure. Other casualties were: Anderson Williams,[41] who was shot in the head at point blank range and killed, a young black man fighting by his side named Peter, and a Mr. Kershaw who was also killed in his home. Kershaw's wife and child, along with a man named Yankee Pierce,[42] made their escapes just before the flaming house collapsed. Col. Gibson also reported that either one or two other men were killed in the Matthew's house.[43] On May 19, 1836, the *Macon Georgia Telegraph* reported that Uriah Horn, the Solicitor for the Chattahoochee Circuit and the commander of the militia company, was also killed at Roanoke.[44] It was later learned that he had survived with serious wounds.[45]

After making his escape, Col. Gibson hid in a nearby spring beneath thick bushes with Indians passing within a few paces as the battle continued. He was later joined in the water by Captain Horne, Elijah Pierce[46] and a Mr. Talbot.

The four men remained hidden until twelve o'clock before leaving the spring. They had only gone as far as the river's bluff when they were met by a party of soldiers hurrying to the relief of the settlement. Col Gibson reached the safety of the town of Lumpkin, Georgia, at sundown that afternoon.[47] Other survivors fled to the safety of the blockhouse at Fort Jones, which was located approximately two miles north of Roanoke.[48]

The Creeks remained at Roanoke about two hours after the battle ended.[49] They evidently returned a short time later, taking possession of the remaining buildings in the town throughout the following week and fortifying themselves in the unburned cotton warehouse while using the town as a ferrying point for people and supplies coming across the Chattahoochee River into Georgia.[50]

Sporadic fighting continued in and around Roanoke for days after the town was destroyed. On May 19th a company of "armed men" from Stewart County arrived at Roanoke. Finding the town occupied by Indians, they charged, killing three Indians and a white man who was with them.[51]

On May 20, 1836, an expedition consisting of mounted militia set out from Columbus, Georgia, with the intent of cutting off the Creeks still holding Roanoke. A second party left the next day and descended the Chattahoochee

River on a steamer. Their plan was to storm the town from the steamer while the mounted militia kept the enemy from escaping by land. They found the town deserted.[52]

Jacob Rhett Motte, a surgeon with the U.S. Army when it arrived at Roanoke in June, notes that for eight miles before they came to the town the road was lined with heaps of ashes. Few of the families who had lived in these homes had escaped without losing some of their family members. When he reached the town, he says not a house was left standing, which may mean that the only remaining cotton warehouse had also been burned after the initial attack on May 15th. Motte and another surgeon pitched their tent on the site of Colonel Gibson's burned home from which soldiers removed the bones of the Donaldson brothers who had been burned to death the night of the attack. On June 24, 1836, two-thousand Georgia Militia, along with General Winfield Scott and his staff, arrived at Roanoke and made camp amid the ruins of the town. The army remained there until June 26th when, under cover of their artillery and expecting to be attacked as they did so, they crossed the Chattahoochee River on rafts. Once they were on the Alabama side of the river, they immediately spotted the tracks of Indian scouts who had been observing them from the riverbank. They were able to pursue and capture one of the scouts who turned out to be a black man living with the Creeks.

Dr. Motte tells of a great amount of devastation the army encountered on the Alabama side of the river. On July 11, after leaving Fort Mitchell, located about thirty miles north of Roanoke, they saw one spot in the road that was filled with empty coffins taken during an attack on a detail sent out to recover the dead for burial.[53]

Some reports claim those killed at Roanoke were buried in a single grave in the Lumpkin Baptist Cemetery and that the grave was covered by a large rock. Other reports say that they were buried in Roanoke Village Cemetery which is located off the Omaha-Georgetown Road.[54]

The news of Roanoke's destruction spread rapidly throughout southern Georgia, Florida, and Alabama creating panic among citizens. Settlers across the three states began to fortify strategic homesteads for use as blockhouses and erect other defensive works. Throughout lower Georgia, requests for arms and ammunition flooded the governor's office. Militia companies were hastily formed. About three weeks after the attack on Roanoke, militia from Stewart and adjoining counties clashed with the Creeks at Shepherd's Plantation in Stewart County. The Creeks were victorious, driving off the militia.[55]

Only July 3, 1836, a large band of Creek

warriors and their families was attacked on an island in the Chickasawhachee Swamp in Baker County, Georgia. The Indians fled after half an hour of battle, leaving behind most of their supplies. One militiaman was killed and fourteen were wounded.[56] This battle was the first defeat of the Creeks and the turning point of the uprising. The remaining Creeks retreated southward, towards the Seminoles in Florida. They were defeated in several battles along the way. On July 10, 1836, a large party of Creeks was attacked by Lowndes County Militia on Brushy Creek in upper Lowndes County, Georgia. Twenty-two Creeks and two blacks were killed and eighteen women and children were captured. Militia losses were three killed and nine wounded.[57]

Following the Battle of Brushy Creek, skirmishing continued in lower Georgia throughout the remainder of 1836. Although the conflict continued in Florida until 1842, with the exception of minor hostilities in the Okefeenokee Swamp area of Georgia in 1838, the Creek War in Georgia was over.

Estimates as to the number of settlers killed and wounded during the attack on Roanoke vary. Col. Gibson claims eight in his account, while the same article states that nine whites were killed in the first onrush and eight or nine others were wounded. An update contained in the same edition of the *Macon*

Georgia Telegraph claims that only "two or three whites" were killed. Captain John Page, in his report to General Gibson, says that seven bodies had been seen by a passerby, while the *Macon Georgia Telegraph* reported nine killed and fifteen missing on May 19, 1836. More modern accounts give anywhere from "most of the inhabitants"[58] to seven, to twelve. The only report of Indian casualties claims that there were three killed.[59]

Taking names and numbers of casualties from the various accounts given after the attack, the following people were known to have been in Roanoke between May 13th and 15th, 1836:

Killed May 15, 1836.

Donaldson, Mr.: Killed in Flex Gibson's home.

Donaldson, Mr.: Killed in Flex Gibson's home.

House, Joseph Turner: Killed in the hotel
(Matthew's home)
Kershaw, Mr.: Killed in his home

Leary, James: A militiaman

McBride, Eleazar.

Peter: A young black man

Toombs, George.

Williams, Anderson

2 unnamed white males: Killed in the Matthew's house (hotel)

3 unnamed blacks" Accounts do not agree to the number killed. It varies between two and five.

The following are known to have been in Roanoke on May 15, 1836, but survived the attack.

Gibson, Felix G.: Slightly wounded

Hardwick, W.M., Dr.: Survived, left the town to return to Major Howard's command Saturday evening.

Horn, Uriah. Severely wounded. He was the militia commander and was originally reported killed.

Kershaw, Mrs.: Survived

Kershaw, ?: Child. Survived.

Pierce, Elijah. Survived

Pierce, Yankee. Survived

Talbot, ?. Survived

Williams, Gazaway. Survived

The above list sets the total killed at fourteen, although the number of black fatalities varies from two to five. Only two people are definitely reported as wounded. Some accounts say the number of wounded was much higher, but do not specify names or numbers. Using the rule of thumb that there are usually more wounded than killed in battle, there could conceivably have been at least twenty wounded. With the complete surprise of the town, the number of wounded may well have been much higher. Colonel Gibson reported eight whites killed plus one black for a total of nine, but does not give the number of wounded. The May 26, 1836, edition of the *Columbus Enquirer* reports that the soldiers who arrived that afternoon found seven whites and five blacks killed plus one man wounded (possibly Captain Horne) and fifteen missing. This may not take into account some of the dead still in the smoldering remains of the houses. It seems logical that the number of whites killed was no less than the eight reported by Col. Gibson. The number of wounded cannot be ascertained by the available information, but the report by the relief column of only one, seems unlikely. Many of the fifteen people reported missing could have been wounded when they were found. No follow up report tells what happened to these fifteen people. It is known from other reports that several of them were blacks who were taken to Alabama by the Indians after the raid.

Using the preceding information, the story of Roanoke can be pieced together with reasonably accuracy.

On Friday, May 13, 1836, Hitachee Indians under the leadership of a half-Indian leader know as Jim Henry, attacked the steamship *Georgian* while it was loading at the town pier. The steamer's crew managed to pull away from the pier and escape down river without serious injuries. The people on the dock scattered. Some fled without looking back and later, panic stricken, relayed the news that the steamer had been taken and the crew killed.[60] The nervous settlers in the area were more than ready to believe this story in light of several skirmishes and ambushes that had occurred in Alabama over the previous few weeks and the newspapers gobbled up the story without questioning its accuracy. Over the course of time, this incorrect version became history.

As the fighting on Friday died down, Creeks scouts quietly probed the settler's hastily improved defense. By Sunday, with no more sightings of hostile Indians, the militia and townspeople relaxed. Many of the militiamen departed to spend Sunday with their families, leaving twenty of their company behind to secure the town. The Creeks immediately took advantage of the situation.

Crossing the river undetected on

Saturday night, May 14, 1836, the warriors found Roanoke lightly defended. Surrounding the town, they crept forward, waiting as the defenders became complacent and tired. Later that night, the pickets, who consisted of undisciplined volunteers with little or no training, decided that there was no danger and quietly slipped back to camp where many promptly fell asleep. The hooting of owls was commented on by some of the militia, but these concerns were lightly brushed away by their comrades with taunts of being scared or jumpy.

Waiting until the town and camp were asleep, three hundred Creek warriors crept silently forward. Stepping lightly past sleeping militia, they posted themselves at the doors and windows of buildings, waiting for the prearranged signal that was given just as dawn brightened the eastern horizon. They began firing through the windows and doors and continued to fire as militiamen and townspeople poured from buildings and scattered towards the safety of the woods. The pickets that Colonel Gibson reported fleeing through the town were militiamen from the camp near one of the cotton warehouses. There may have been no pickets still on their posts, unless they had awakened early and were making their way back to their positions. The defenders did manage to return fire as they retreated, yet overall, there was no sustained defense.

With the militia routed, the Indians commenced looting the town, taking what they could carry and burning all the buildings except for one cotton warehouse. About two hours later, they re-crossed the river with their plunder and captives. The captives were slaves that the Creeks regularly appropriated as their own throughout the war. Many of these became slaves to Indian masters; others became allies and members of the tribe through adoption or marriage. With the departure of the Creeks, the survivors began creeping from their hiding places. They were found by the relief force that arrived around noon.

About seven hundred and fifty people lived at Roanoke. Of those, about seventy were actually in the town on the morning of the attack. Strictly speaking, Roanoke wasn't a massacre, but it was a Pyrrhic victory for the Creeks. Jim Henry, the leader of the attacking Creeks, was pursued to Florida, fighting several skirmishes along the way. He escaped after a clash with militia at Notchaway Creek on July 27, 1836, but was eventually taken into custody and carried to the Indian Territory in Oklahoma where he became a Methodist minister of the gospel.[61]

Roanoke was never rebuilt. The survivors moved a few miles north, where they founded the village of Liverpool. Today, this town is known as Florence, Georgia and it is the site of a marina that serves the lake that now covers the original site of Roanoke.

On August 6, 1931, the Roanoke Chapter of the DAR unveiled a historical marker at Roanoke. The names of those slain on May 15, 1836, were affixed on a bronze plaque. Today, the site is partially underwater due to the damming of the Chattahoochee River and the creation of Lake Eufaula. The extreme eastern portion of the area is under cultivation. The site is all but obliterated. Sometimes a post or nail may be found when the water is low. The concrete pillar installed by the DAR is no longer visible. It is either underwater or has been removed by unknown persons. At present, it seems likely that Roanoke will remain forgotten.

WORKS CITED

Cooper, Walter G. 1938. <u>The Story of Georgia.</u> Vol. 3. New York: The American Historical Society, Inc.

Debo, Angie. 1941. <u>A History of the Creek Indians.</u> Norman: University of Oklahoma Press.

Dixon, Sara Robertson. 1975. <u>The History of Stewart County, Georgia.</u> Columbus: Columbus Office Supply Company.

Granberry, Joseph John. 1889. <u>Reminiscence No. 1 – The Burning of Roanoke.</u> Americus: Americus Daily Republican. 24 March 1889.

Huxford, Folks. 1949. <u>The History of Brooks County, Georgia.</u> Athens: The McGregor Company.

Krakow, Kenneth. 1975 <u>Georgia Place Names.</u> Macon: the Winship Press.

Meltzer, Milton. 1972 <u>Hunted Like the Wolf: The Story of the Seminole War.</u> New York: Farrar, Straus, and Giroux.

Motte, Jacob Rhett. 1953. Journey into the
        Wilderness. Ed. James F.
        Sunderman. Gainesville: The
        University of Florida Press.

Page, John. 1836. Letter to [Brigadier General
        George Gibson] Atlanta: State of
        Georgia Archives.

Sherwood, Adel. 1837. A Gazetteer of the
        State of Georgia. Washington City.

Terrill, Helen Eliza. 1958. The History of
        Stewart County, Georgia. vol. 1 & 2.
        Columbus: Columbus Office Supply
        Company.

_____ . 1973. Georgia Historical
        Markers. Valdosta: Bay Tree Grove
        Publishers.

Macon Georgia Telegraph. 19 May 1836, 26
        May 1836
The Columbus Enquirer. (Georgia) 20 May
        1836, 26 May 1836, 26 May 1840.

Georgia Messenger. (Macon) 26 May 1836.

Other Books by G.G. Stokes, Jr.

Non-fiction

Camp Toccoa: First Home of the Airborne.

Between 1942 and 1944 the first United States paratroopers were trained on an isolated base located just outside a Northeast Georgia town.

Historical Fiction

Letters For Catherine:
A Novel of Charleston During the American Revolution

When seventeen-year-old William Hunter marches off to war in the spring of 1780, the Glorious Cause of the American Revolution seems all but lost. Many of the largest cities in his new country are occupied by the forces of King George III, and the noose is tightening around the city of Charleston, South Carolina. Leaving Bethesda Orphanage with nothing more than a kiss from Catherine DeLoach, William sets out to defend his country. His dreams of victory and glory are quickly smashed by the realities of war as he finds that he has enlisted in a desperate struggle against the most powerful empire in the world. Taken prisoner at the fall of Charleston, William is imprisoned on the infamous prison ship, Packhorse. There his hopes and dreams are kept alive only through the letters he writes to Catherine, the beautiful Huguenot girl who waved him off to war with nothing more than a simple kiss and a promise he will keep at all costs.

A Lesser Form of Patriotism:
A Novel of the King's Carolina Rangers and the American Revolution in the South.

It is said that during the American Revolution, more American's served in the British forces than in the Continental Army of the United States. This is their story. In this frontier war, there is no Valley Forge, no Saratoga, no Yorktown. It evolves into a struggle that pits brother against brother, and neighbor against neighbor. The heroes and heroines are simple people who believed in their cause as fervently as did those Americans who fought to free themselves from English rule. A Lesser Form of Patriotism tells their story of love, death, courage, loyalty, and defeat as it chronicles the end of a way of life that began when the first English foot stepped ashore in the New World and ended with the closing shots of the American Revolution.

The Road to Bloody Marsh:
A Novel of King George's War

A chance encounter thrusts a young frontiersman into a world at war when he befriends the son of an English Lord and a French Countess in 1730's Savannah, Georgia. From the streets of Savannah to the frontiers of the new colony, to the Spanish held fortress of St. Augustine, The Road to Bloody Marsh is a spellbinding and fast-paced tale of King George's War as seen through the eyes of three men. Rivals, from rival empires: Geraldo Garzon, the Spaniard whose first loyalty lies with himself; Cyrus Roquemore, the Frenchman who serves two masters; and Morgan Stokes, the Englishman who risks everything to win the heart of the woman he loves.

Loving Lynn Celia:
A Novel of the French and Indian War on the Southern Frontier

In March, 1756, Lynn Celia Claxton arrives in the British colony of Georgia; within a month, she finds herself widowed and on the run from the law.

Stowing away aboard a flatboat on the Savannah River, she is discovered by Thomas Simpson, a young man whose destiny will be intertwined with hers from that moment forward.

From the colonial town of Savannah, to the frontier outpost of Ninety-Six, and into the untamed Carolina mountains, this bittersweet historical novel follows the lives of Thomas and Lynn Celia as they struggle to carve a place for themselves in the hostile and unforgiving wilderness of the colonial Southeast.

Crime / Fiction

Fireson Bay

When the body of a Police Officer is discovered on the banks of Georgia's Chattahoochee River, Special Agent Fireson Bay is called to the scene. There he meets Doctor Lucretia (Creasy) Cook, the coroner for the small Georgia county in which the body is found.

Almost immediately, it becomes apparent that they are dealing with something more sinister than the murder of one man, they are dealing with a serial killer that targets police officers – one, it seems, every five years.

Will Fireson be the next victim, or will the case unravel when the evidence they uncover points to the most unlikely suspect imaginable?

ENDNOTES

[1] Kenneth Krakow, Georgia Place Names. (Macon: The Winship Press, 1975), 193.

[2] Ibid.

[3] Folks Huxford, The History of Brooks County, Georgia. (Athens: The McGregor Company, 1949), 36-37.

[4] Helen Eliza Terrill, History of Stewart County, Georgia. Vol. 1 (Columbus: Columbus Office Supply Co., 1958), 43.

[5] Ibid., 363.

[6] Krakow, 193.

[7] Sherwood, Adel. 1837. A Gazetteer of the State of Georgia. Washington City: p. 219.

[8] The Macon Telegraph, 26 May 1836, p.7.

[9] Terrill calls this business Rood and Peak, but Gibson, in his firsthand account, calls it Rood and Seymour's. It was owned by Ansel Philander Rood and a Mr. Reed. Ansel Rood became a posthumous son-in-law of Felix Gibson when he married Mr. Gibson's daughter in July 1842. Terrill, 475.

[10] Georgia Historical Markers, (Valdosta: Bay Tree Grove Publishers, 1973), 437.

[11] This business was owned by Willoughby Dikes Hill. Terrill, 497.

[12] This business was owned by James Purdie Mathews. Terrill, 364-65. He was also an ensign in the Stewart County Guards, the local militia unit. Terrill, 65.

[13] Sara Robertson Dixon, History of Stewart County, Georgia. (Columbus: Columbus Office Supply Company, 1975), 29.

[14] The Columbus Enquirer, (Georgia) 26 May 1840, p. 2.

[15] Jacob Rhett Motte, Journey into the Wilderness, (Gainesville: University of Florida Press, 1953), 11.

[16] Angie Debo, A History of the Creek Indians. (Norman: the University of Oklahoma Press, 1941), 101.

[17] John Page, Fort Mitchell, Alabama, to [Brigadier General George Gibson], 16 May 1836. State of Georgia Archives, Atlanta, Ga.

[18] Terrill, 43.

[19] In his journal, Motte describes the crossing of the Chattahoochee River at Roanoke. He says that the army crossed on rafts, taking some 18 wagons with them. He notes only that the current was swift and the opposite banks were steep, but does not mention any major difficulties encountered in the crossing. Motte, 15.

[20] Georgia Messenger, (Macon) 2 June 1836, p. 2

[21] Both Eneah Micco and Eneah Mathla were captured during a raid that was made on their camp in Alabama by militia under the command of General Jesup. Both men were shipped to the Indian Territories in Oklahoma. Motte, 253.

[22] In contrast to these numbers, the hostile forces had few warriors. The 300 that attacked Roanoke probably represented the majority of their entire fighting force. Motte, 253.

[23] Motte, 248.

[24] Milton Meltzer, Hunted Like the Wolf: The Story of the Seminole War. (New York: Farrar, Straus, and Giroux, 1972), 123.

[25] Macon Georgia Telegraph, 19 May 1836, p.3.

[26] Walter G. Cooper, The Story of Georgia, Vol. 3, (New York: the American Historical Society, Inc. , 1938.), 292.

[27] John Page, Fort Mitchell, Alabama, to [Brigadier General George Gibson], 16 May 1836. State of Georgia Archives, Atlanta, Ga.

[28] The Columbus Enquirer, (Georgia) 26 May 1836, p. 2.

[29] Huxford, 36.

[30] Macon Georgia Telegraph, 19 May 1836, p.3.

[31] Dixon, 28.

[32] The Macon Georgia Telegraph, 26 May 1836, p. 6.

[33] Columbus Enquirer, (Georgia) 26 May 1840, p. 2.

[34] Ibid.

[35] In his journal, Motte notes the inclination of the militia to sleep while on guard duty. He reports that on finding one of the militia guards asleep, the man told him that he had a tooth ache that prevented him from staying awake. Motte volunteered to be an officer of the guard because he did not trust his safety to the militia sentries. Motte, 15.

[36] Dixon, 30.

[37] Terrill, 43.

[38] Terrill, 364 says the attack took place at approximately 2 AM.

[39] Felix G. Gibson (1795-1841) was one of the earliest settlers in Roanoke. After he arrived in the area in 1831 he built a home and, along with two of his brother-in-laws, Anderson and Gazaway Williams, he opened one of the large cotton warehouses in the town. Terrill, 974.

[40] Motte, 12.

[41] Anderson Williams was the brother-in-law of Col. Gibson whose eyewitness account follows in the text. Terrill, 474.

[42] Dixon, 31.

[43] Terrill, in her History of Stewart County, tells this story. The two men, finding there was no escape, concealed themselves in the chimney where they were burned to death when the house was consumed by flames. Terrill, 364.

[44] The Macon Georgia Telegraph. 19 May 1836. p. 3.

[45] Ibid., 7.

[46] Dixon, Vol. 1, 30.

[47] The Macon Georgia Telegraph, 26 May 1836, p. 7.

[48] Georgia Historical Markers. (Valdosta: Bay Tree Grove Publishers, 1973.) , 437.

[49] Georgia Messenger, (Macon) 2 June 1836, p. 2.

[50] The Macon Georgia Telegraph, 26 May 1836, p. 7.

[51] Columbus Enquirer. (Georgia) 20 May 1836, p. 2.

[52] The Macon Georgia Telegraph, 26 May 1836, p. 7.

[53] Motte, 11-21

[54] Dixon, Vol. 2, 420

[55] Huxford, 37.

[56] Huxford, 38.

[57] Huxford, 40.

[58] Krakow, 193.

[59] Motte, 251.

[60] In his journal, Motte gives an example of this mentality on page 8, which shows how the mere sight of Indians could cause great alarm. "By sunrise we were again on the march (to Roanoke), and continued it uninterrupted until noon, when a Negro was seen running after us with the speed of the wind, terror depicted in every feature. "The Indians! The Indians!" cried he; well what of them?" "Dem coming up de road arter you fass." What do they look like? "Like de berry debble; demheap, and all naked." Naked Indians; that could not be Paddy Carr's band, whom we expected to follow us; and the hostile Indians are known to fight naked. "Semper paratus" is the safest principle of action; so our men were drawn up in battle array across the road. This band of "hostiles" turned out to be Paddy Carr's band of about one-hundred friendly Creek scouts who were hurrying to join the main column of troops. Motte, 8.

[61] Dixon, 35.

Notes

www.ingramcontent.com/pod-product-compliance
Lightning Source LLC
Chambersburg PA
CBHW070050040426
42331CB00034B/2962